SCHOOL

IN MY LIFETIME

Written by
Rebecca Phillips-Bartlett

sales@northstareditions.com
888-417-0195

Library of Congress Control Number:
The Library of Congress Control Number is available on the Library of Congress website.

ISBN
979-8-89359-326-6 (library bound)
979-8-89359-410-2 (paperback)
979-8-89359-382-2 (epub)
979-8-89359-356-3 (hosted ebook)

Printed in the United States of America
Mankato, MN
092025

Written by:
Rebecca Phillips-Bartlett

Edited by:
Alex Hall

Designed by:
Jasmine Pointer

All facts, statistics, web addresses and URLs in this book were verified as valid and accurate at time of writing. No responsibility for any changes to external websites or references can be accepted by either the author or publisher.

Image Credits

Images courtesy of Shutterstock.com, unless otherwise stated.

Cover – Valeriya_Dor, Andrew Rybalko. Throughout – Andrew Rybalko. 6–7 – val lawless. 8–9 – BonNontawat, BrunoWeltmann, Tally18. 10–11 – Education StockPhoto, Maryville University Archives, CC0, via Wikimedia Commons, chuyuss. 12–13 – Roman Nerud, Karolis Kavolelis, Paket, By Carol M. Highsmith - Library of CongressCatalog, via Wikimedia Commons. 14–15 – Sashkin, SpicyTruffel, 19 STUDIO, Esgoty, KIKUCHI. 16–17 – the8monkey, Esgoty, strekalova, Gorodenkoff, Maryna Stryhun. 18–19 – Kaspars Grinvalds, Hung Chung Chih, Evgeny Karandaev. 20–21 – kichikimi. 22–23 – Mariana Hihiieva, eamesBot.

CONTENTS

Words that look like this can be found in the glossary on page 24.

BACK IN MY DAY

Layla felt like she had been working on her math project for hours already. Eventually, the doorbell rang.

Caleb rushed to the door to let Nana in.

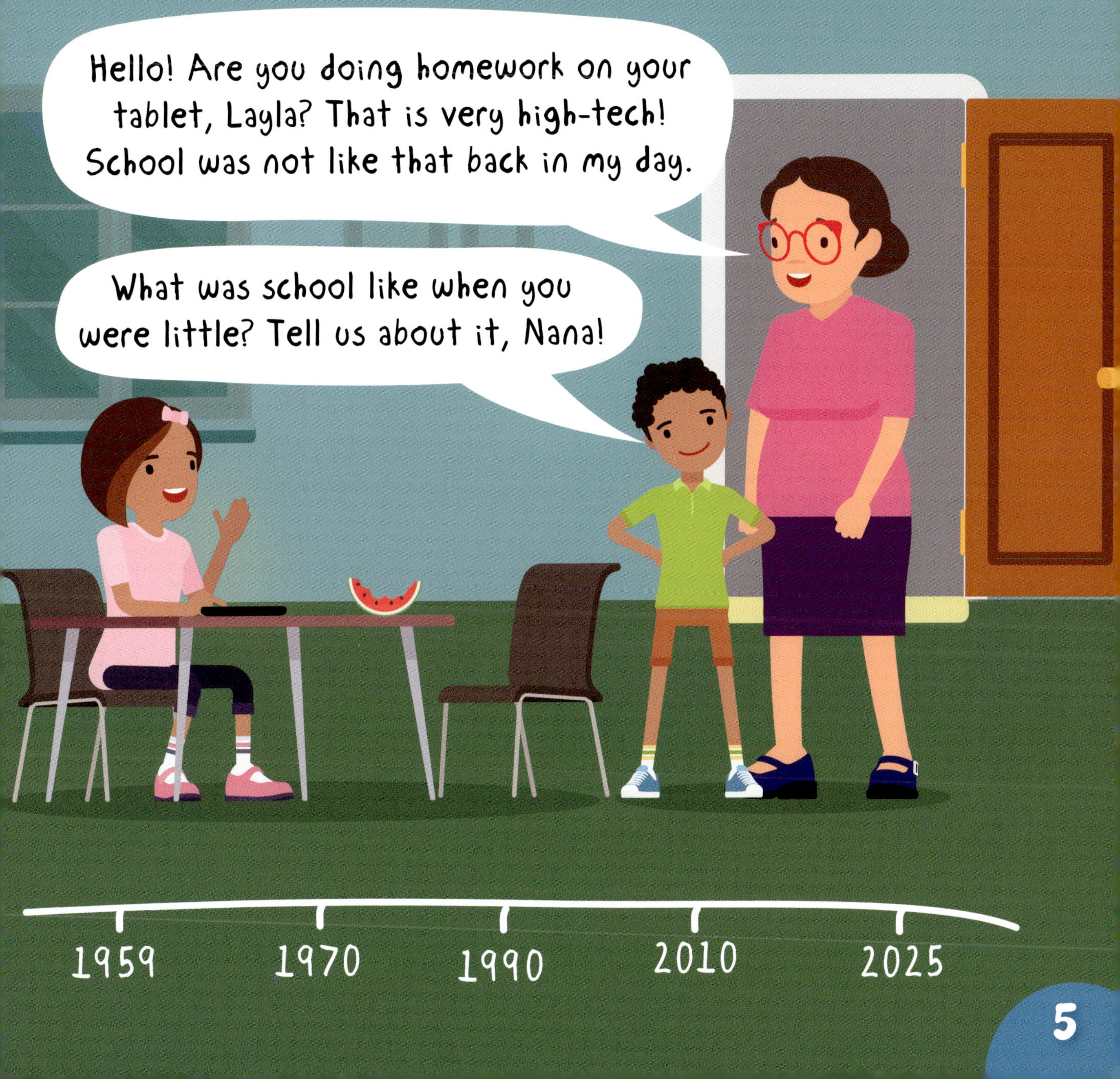

WHEN I WAS BORN

In the 1950s and 1960s, most young children did not go to preschool. They stayed at home and learned from their parents.

What toys did you play with as a baby?
How did they help you learn?

WHEN I WAS YOUNG

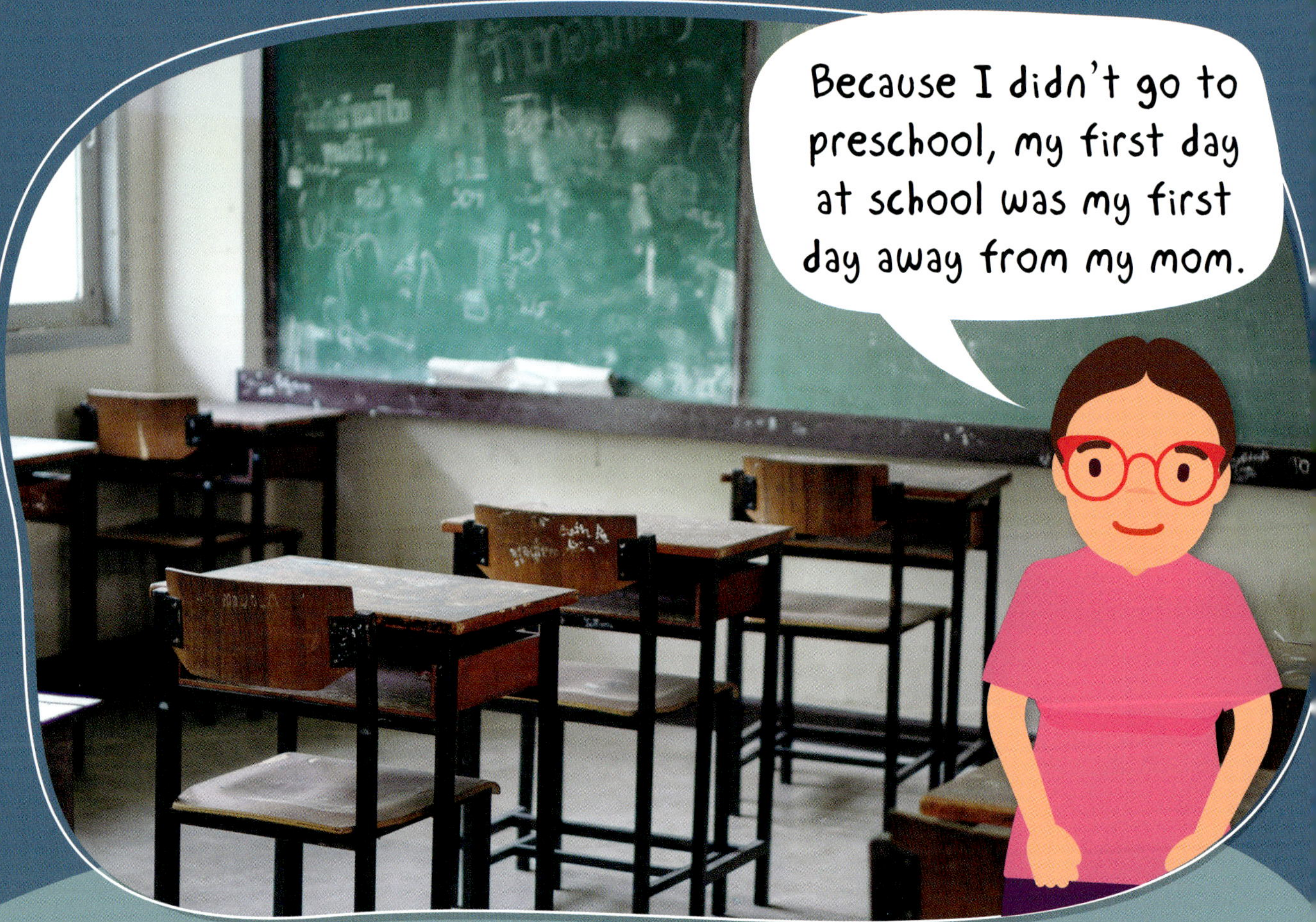

Nana started school in 1964 when she was five years old. Her classroom was made up of rows of wooden desks.

At the front of the classroom, the teacher wrote on a chalkboard for everyone to see.

Nana graduated high school in 1977 when she was 18 years old.

Overhead projectors used see-through sheets of paper and a light-up box. The teacher could write on the paper and zoom in on important parts.

I REMEMBER...

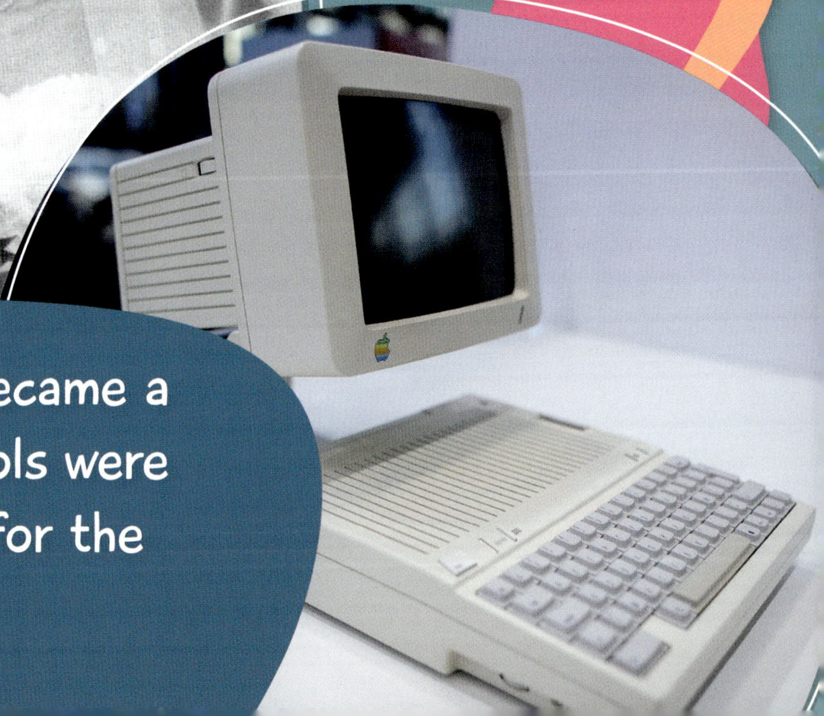

By the time Nana became a teacher, some schools were getting computers for the children to use.

Once a week, I took my class to the school's computer room. The children learned how to type on the computer. Unlike now, my students didn't have computers, tablets, or smartphones at home. Typing was a brand-new skill.

Wow! Computers have been around for my whole life, so I don't remember learning to type.
We were still getting used to computers back then. Not so long before this, programmers were some of the only people who knew how to use computers.

In 1953, computers were programmed using symbols. Then, a woman called Grace Hopper suggested using words to program computers instead.

Grace Hopper

Grace Hopper invented a new computer language. Her language meant more and more people could learn how to use computers.

HOW VERY MODERN!

By the 2000s, computers were a regular part of many schools. Chalkboards had been replaced by whiteboards.

In 2005, my classroom got an <u>interactive</u> whiteboard. I could plug my laptop into the board and show my class what was on the screen. It felt very <u>modern</u>!

We have an interactive whiteboard in my class!

So do I!

NOWADAYS...

Nowadays, all sorts of devices are used in our classrooms to help us learn.

Lots of homework apps and websites help us practice what we have learned.

We can use the internet to find out more about our favorite topics.

However, lots of older inventions are still important today too!

Pens, pencils, and paper have been around for a very long time. We still use these things every day.

Books continue to be a great way to learn more and become a master of reading.

NANA'S TIMELINE

1964—Nana started school. Her school had a chalkboard.

1960—Nana played with wooden blocks and was read to by her parents.

1959—Nana was born.

1977—Nana graduated high school and went to college to become a teacher. She used overhead projectors.

1982—Nana and Gramps got married. Nana started working as a teacher.

1984—Nana's school got its first computers.

2005—Nana's classroom got an interactive whiteboard.

TOMORROW'S WORLD

Lots of things are invented all the time. Many inventions are made to solve problems, help people, or make things easier.

Do you prefer writing using devices, such as computers and tablets, or by hand using pens or pencils? What could you invent to change school life?

What would YOU invent?

GLOSSARY

apps programs that work on devices such as smartphones to allow them to do different things

devices machines or inventions made to do something

graduated finished a training course or school

interactive when someone or something, such as a computer, responds to something the user does

invented when something new is created for the first time

modern to do with recent or present times

programmers people whose jobs are to make computer programs, which make computers able to do certain things

INDEX